Better Homes and Gardens®

FINISHING TOUCHES

TABLE OF CONTENTS

CREATIVE WALLS
Artful Appliqué 4
Combed-On Texture. 6
Sponged-On Romance 8
Stenciled Antiquity 10

PAINTED FLOORS
Snappy Checks 12
Nostalgic Hearts 14

FURNITURE FINISHES
Faux Marble 16
Cottage Classics 18
Rejuvenated Metal 20

PERSONALITY PROJECTS
Easy Accents 22

Really great rooms have one thing in common: a spark of individuality that simply can't be bought at a furniture store. How do you get it? Adapt the personality-adding decorating projects on these pages. From easy furniture fix-ups to artful wall treatments, there's something here for every skill and taste.

ARTFUL APPLIQUÉ

As if cloaked in peeling birch bark, the walls of this dining area belie their humble origin.

A clever covering of torn paper, ingeniously applied over a plain wall, creates a gently textured background for a mix of natural wood furnishings. As rich and homespun as it is light and airy, the papered facade lends log-cabin character, without the expected heaviness.

To achieve the look, white kraft paper with brown backing was pasted to the walls. Next, strips of the paper were peeled back carefully to reveal irregular slashes of the brown back side.

Kraft paper, the stuff of shopping bags and cardboard box sheathing, comes in various finishes and thicknesses. Look for kraft paper at art supply stores or local bag companies.

Begin by tearing the kraft paper into wide strips. Next, apply the strips to the wall with heavy wallpaper paste, overlapping the edges as needed.

Let the paper dry, then start peeling to create the loglike design. Don't worry about perfection; the irregularity of the peeled patches is essential to the rustic look.

You can achieve a similar look by painting your walls a medium-tan color, then applying a collage of white paper pieces.

COMBED-ON TEXTURE

A rich blend of color and design, this striated wall treatment brings high style to any plain space. Best of all, even a novice can create the look.

Want a patterned wall without the fuss (and permanence) of wallpaper? Comb it! One of the easiest painted effects to achieve, this treatment involves dragging a comblike tool through wet paint. Here's how to do it.

Although the paint color and intensity depend on your taste, think about the room's natural light when making your decision. Reduce glare in sunny south- or west-facing rooms with cool blues, greens, or mauves. Or, lighten an inherently dark space, like this dining room, with glowing yellow tones.

Start by rolling on a semigloss or high-gloss paint, then letting it dry for 48 hours.

Next, make your combing tool by cutting notches in sturdy cardboard or acetate, or—as in this room—by notching a rubber-edged dustpan. Working on one wall at at time, apply flat paint and quickly "comb it." This is best done by two people working together, one applying the paint and the other creating the design. Don't worry about making straight lines; undulations and imperfections enhance the handmade charm.

Easy and versatile, combing can produce virtually limitless effects. Practice variations on cardboard, then choose the look you like. Consider layering different colors and creating cross-hatched or diagonal designs. Or, use combing to make up for your room's architectural defects. "Raise" a low ceiling with vertical stripes, or add the illusion of width to a small room with horizontal lines.

SPONGED-ON ROMANCE

Like soft water-colors, sponged-on patterns enrich contemporary settings with aged character and subtle dimension.

Why paint on a flat color when you can wrap your room with romance. Surprisingly airy and translucent, three softly dabbed colors—pink, peach, and cream—produce a layered, dimensional look that expands space in this living room.

The colors you choose depend on the mood you want to convey. In general, opt for light colors, using pastels for flowery romance, and neutral alabaster, beige, and grays for cool, marblelike effects.

Sponging requires only a few easy-to-find materials. You'll need a piece of natural sea sponge for each color you'll be applying. (One-third to one-half of a sponge works well. Avoid synthetic sponges, which will not produce richly textured impressions.)

Plan for one plate or pan (disposable pie plates are ideal)

for dipping each sponge. Finally, use at least three colors of latex or oil-base paint—a base coat and two or more additional colors for your sponged designs.

Practice your technique and test your colors on a piece of cardboard or scrap wood to be sure the effect is what you have in mind. First, paint your walls the base color of your choice; let them dry thoroughly.

On top of the base shade, you can sponge as many colors as you wish. Start by dipping a sponge lightly into paint and pressing it to the wall. Space the patches of color as evenly as possible, but change the position of the sponge frequently to achieve an irregular, mottled effect.

When the surface is dry, apply the second color, using separate sponges for each shade. Concentrate on blank spots, but overlap the prints, as well. Repeat the process for each additional color.

Stenciled Antiquity

Once viewed as a low-cost substitute for wallpaper, stenciling today is valued as an art form in its own right. Happily, novices can quickly master the skill.

Consider the possibilities! Whether you start with ready-made stencils or cut your own motifs from stencil paper, you can assemble any mix of patterns and colors you like. Dot a wall with hearts and flowers, or create instant architecture by stenciling a frieze at the ceiling line. The main ingredient: your creativity.

You will need stencils, stencil brushes, and paints. Stencils from paint and crafts stores come in many styles, from authentic reproductions of colonial patterns to contemporary motifs. Or, you can cut your own from stencil paper available at crafts stores. You can use ordinary wall paint, although fast-drying acrylic paints are ideal for stenciling.

The secret to successful stenciling is a nearly dry brush. Once you've anchored your stencil with masking tape at the corners, dip the tip of the brush into the paint. Remove excess paint by pushing the bristles up and down on newspapers. Now, dab—don't brush—the paint through the stencil, holding the brush perpendicular to the stencil and using an up-and-down motion to apply the paint. (If you stroke or drag your brush across the stencil, you risk creating smears under the edges.)

Work from the sides of the stencil toward the center. When done, carefully lift off the stencil and continue.

As you work toward a room's boundaries (a corner, for instance), you may need to stretch or shorten the last link or two, or plan some extra spacing to avoid awkwardly cutting off the design. (With the motif shown here, for example, that would mean widening, compressing, or spacing out one or more leaf-and-flower units.)

SNAPPY CHECKS

Don't let your walls have all the fun! Indoors or out, you probably have a neglected wood floor that's begging for a little artful attention.

Traditional colonial checks look surprisingly fresh and contemporary these days. Shown here on a porch floor, this checkerboard "rug" awakens a small sitting spot. Durable deck paint ensures longevity.

Sand the floor to "rough up" the old finish, prime any bare spots, and let dry overnight.

Mark the perimeter of the rug on the floor, using a pencil and a metal yardstick. Tape the edges with masking tape, paint the rug area white, and let dry.

Follow the design as pictured (or vary it to suit your taste), and draw the pattern over the white paint. To establish straight lines, fasten lengths of string with tape from one side of the design to the other.

Select several patches from the rug that are not adjacent to each other; tape them off and paint them with gray deck paint. Pull the tape away and let the paint dry thoroughly. Repeat for several more patches using more gray paint. Repeat again and again until all of the gray patches are filled.

When the design is completed and dry, touch up the lines as needed with an artist's brush.

Use tape to mask off simple diagonal stripes. Or, paint your rug a solid color, then mask off and color in one large central diamond. For fun, dip the tip of a 1-inch brush into paint and dab on some phony fringe.

NOSTALGIC HEARTS

Be bold! Brush on a colorful room-size "carpet," a stairway runner, or an area "rug." Several coats of polyurethane over the paint create long wear.

Bright colors, crisp designs, and nostalgic hearts add up to modern romance. Here, the combination turns a once-dull kitchen dining area into an inviting gathering spot.

Repeating designs, like this heart rug, make it easy to adapt your handiwork to any size space. Simply add or subtract rows of hearts as needed.

To fashion your own design, you'll need a steady hand, masking tape or stencils, and paint. Just mask off simple shapes, like squares and stripes, buy ready-made stencils at paint and crafts stores, or make your own personalized cutouts in commercial stencil paper.

Prepare the floor by removing any old wax, then sand the area

to be painted. Protect bare wood with a coat of oil-base primer and let dry. Paint your base coat, using two or three coats of oil-base paint (either flat or shiny deck paint).

To create the designs, brush paint (oil-base or acrylic) between masked lines, or dab the paint through stencils. Let it dry.

Apply three to five coats of polyurethane varnish. Let each coat dry overnight before applying the next.

Sprinkle stenciled flowers or leaves randomly over a floor for subtle romance. Or, paint on a solid, checked, or floral 12-inch-wide border.

FAUX MARBLE

Transform a has-been table or chair into a marbleized masterpiece. Sponged-on paints and randomly drawn veining create the look.

Start with a garage-sale bargain, then have some fun and dab on the colors. Although you can use this table as a guide, don't worry about copying its designs and colors exactly. After all, even natural marble comes in a variety of patterns and hues.

Before you attempt the real thing, practice on a piece of cardboard or scrap wood to test your technique and color mix.

Sand the furniture piece, wiping away any loose particles, and brush on a coat of white primer. Let dry.

Next, randomly brush on your mix of colors, using a different brush for each color. Pink, white, gray, and mossy green were applied to this piece. Apply the paint to a small area at a time— an area about the size of one-third of this tabletop or a 15-inch-square patch.

Immediately, take a piece of natural sea sponge or crumpled newspaper and dab lightly, swirling the edges of the colors into one another for a mottled-marble effect.

Repeat the same process until the entire piece is painted. As you blot the paint, be sure not to smooth it so much that the colors run together. Let the piece dry.

Take a small, thin artist's brush and apply veining in different colors. Here, both white and gray veins were added.

COTTAGE CLASSICS

Painted furniture has moved into its own in design circles—and for good reason. Homespun yet chic, it sends a comforting down-home message.

Many paths lead to country style. Add farmhouse charm to secondhand wooden pieces with humble white paint, or cozy up a contemporary chest of drawers with colonial-style vinegar painting. (Think of it as finger painting for adults.)

A popular element even in new country pieces, white paint adorns pieces with chunky, turned legs and scrolly carving. Scout secondhand stores and garage sales (or rummage through your own attic) for candidates. The rest is easy: Glue

any loose veneers and apply wood filler where needed. Let dry and sand until smooth. For a good finish, spray the furniture piece with two or more coats of glossy white enamel.

Start by painting the piece with white semigloss enamel. (If you're using an unfinished piece, prime the raw wood and let it dry.) Sand when dry and wipe with white vinegar. To make the vinegar paint: Mix ¼ cup white vinegar, ½ teaspoon sugar, and 3 drops dishwashing liquid. In another container, mix 2 tablespoons dry powdered tempera paint with enough vinegar solution to make a paste; continue adding the vinegar solution until the paste becomes creamy. Apply vinegar paint with a brush. Press dry objects onto the surface, lifting the vinegar paint off. (We used a fingertip to make rows of dots and a terry towel to create the squiggly lines.) Let dry. Protect with two coats of varnish.

REJUVENATED METAL

Vintage metal beds are back in style. Slicked up with fresh color, they combine nostalgic lines with '80s pizzazz.

It's easy to be seduced by the charm of an old metal bed. Take time to choose and repaint your special find.

When considering an old bed, be sure it has the original bed frame. In the past, every metal bed was made and fitted together individually, not mass-produced. A headboard and footboard will probably have to be tailored to fit an unmatched frame, which can cost you more than the old bed itself.

Next, ask yourself how strong and stable the bed is. Examine the bed just as you would wood furniture; it should feel heavy, decorative parts should be cast, and all the joints should fit solidly together. Finally, be sure that the bed is sturdy. If it rattles in the store or auction house, it will rattle and squeak at home.

It takes little more than time and patience to refinish a metal bed. Here are the four steps to successful results:
- Remove the old paint with a paint remover. (Wear rubber gloves and work in a well-ventilated place.) To be sure all of the paint has been loosened, leave the remover on for the recommended length of time. Repeated as needed.
- After removing the paint, sand the bed well to ensure that the primer adheres to the metal.
- Prime all surfaces with any type of commercial primer.
- After the primer has dried, spray- or brush-paint the metal bed with several light coats of enamel. If you use a brush, spread the enamel quickly to avoid brush marks.

*E*ASY ACCENTS

Turn a blank wall or dull corner into an eye-catching accent with an inventive screen or mirror.

Give your imagination free reign when it comes to accessorizing your home. Let a cleverly painted screen wake up a plain corner or hide a radiator. Or, turn that featureless entryway or living room wall into a knockout focal point with a neoclassic mirror (of surprising origin). Either project will lend decorating punch to your place.

Start with an arched-top mirror, readily available from large mail-order catalogs. It takes only an hour and some tape from an art-supply store to turn the mirror into a neoclassic "window."

Start by measuring off your small "panes" and outlining them with lengths of black tape. Overlap 1-inch snips of tape to make smoothly rounded lines.

The pilasters? They're made of ordinary lumber and round plastic plumbing caps.

Artful? Yes. Difficult? No! Make this screen by cutting fiberboard into four pieces, then drill holes 6 inches apart. Paint the panels with two coats of white paint and let dry. Mask off geometric patterns and spray the panels blue. When the paint is dry, peel off the masking tape. For a grand finale, sprinkle the panels with red paint drops. To assemble, just use book rings from an office-supply store.

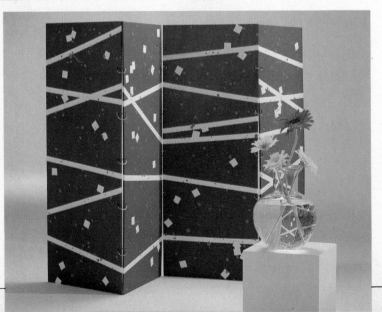

ACKNOWLEDGMENTS

Page 4
Design: Leo Adams

Page 6
Design: Ilene Sanford and David Michel

Page 8
Design: Richard Kaleh

Page 10
Design: John Houser

Page 12
Design: Rebecca Jerdee

Page 14
Design: Christine H. Bakalar

Page 16
Design: Becky Franco

Page 22
Screen design: Robert E. Dittmer

Page 23
Mirror design: Denise L. Caringer